the PARACLETE BOOK *of*

HOSPITALITY

THE EDITORS *of* PARACLETE PRESS

the PARACLETE BOOK *of*

HOSPITALITY

PARACLETE PRESS
BREWSTER, MASSACHUSETTS

The Paraclete Book of Hospitality

2012 First Printing

Copyright © 2012 by Paraclete Press, Inc.

ISBN: 978-1-55725-665-2

All scriptural references unless otherwise marked are taken from the *New Revised Standard Version of the Bible,* copyright 1989, 1995 by the Division of Christian Education of the National Council of Churches of Christ in the United States of America and are used by permission. All rights reserved.

Quotations referenced as KJV are taken from the authorized *King James Version* of the Bible.

Quotations referenced as NJB are taken from the *New Jerusalem Bible,* copyright © 1985 by Darton, Longman & Todd, Ltd. and Doubleday, a division of Random House, Inc. Reprinted by permission.

Quotations referenced as REB are taken from the *Revised English Bible,* copyright © 1989 by Oxford University Press and Cambridge University Press. Reprinted by permission.

Library of Congress Cataloging-in-Publication Data
The Paraclete book of hospitality / created by the editors of Paraclete Press.
     p. cm.
  Includes bibliographical references (p.   ).
  ISBN 978-1-55725-665-2 (trade pbk.)
  1. Hospitality—Religious aspects—Christianity. I. Paraclete Press.
  BV4647.H67P37 2012
  241'.671—dc23   2011051892

10 9 8 7 6 5 4 3 2 1

Published by Paraclete Press
Brewster, Massachusetts
www.paracletepress.com
Printed in the United States of America

A Prayer for Hospitality

Dear gracious and loving God,
Help me see what I don't sometimes see.
Show me needs and how I might meet them.
Give me your love in extraordinary measure,
And then guide me how and where to express it.
When I share my table, my home, or my life, bless me
with your bounty.
For what I have is yours; and what
I give to others
Is you.
Amen.

CONTENTS

How to Use This Book

Hospitality is many things. It is the work of soup kitchens and neighborhood parties. It is the way we open ourselves up to others and share the light of Christ with friends and strangers.

Is there anything more beautiful than the meeting of friends, the sharing of burdens, the genuine love for another human being? Perhaps there is. Perhaps it is even more beautiful, in the Christian worldview, when these things happen between those who are not friends—between strangers extending beyond their comfort zones to become friends, listening and helping in times of trouble, showing love in tangible ways. For a follower of Jesus, *this* is the most beautiful way of life.

It can be tough to do!

Learning to appreciate and then practice hospitality involves a combination of acquiring or honing skills, of discovering or accepting God's gifts and grace, of learning from the experiences of others, of listening, and of developing certain habits. All of these aspects will be reflected in the pages that follow.

You may already be a pro at this essential Christian work. Or you may find it very difficult. Hospitality is God's graciousness, expressed in and through us. Hospitality is an opportunity to be like Christ—what a gift!

We present this book to you out of our own lives, our own attempts, struggles, and small successes in practicing Christian hospitality. The mission of Paraclete Press is grounded in the Benedictine tradition of monastic spiritual practice. Nearly everyone who works at Paraclete is a member of an ecumenical Christian community known as The Community of Jesus. Here we gather throughout the day to pray the Daily Office. Most of us live together with other families and single people in the Community. We share our homes—living together in the nitty-gritty of our daily lives. We eat meals together and share the responsibilities involved in caring for our homes, our place of worship, and for each other. We still fail much of the time, but we have worked hard over the years at trying to be hospitable in the ways of Jesus, as expressed in the Benedictine tradition. We are intentional about hospitality. So in this book we are sharing with you what we've learned from our successes and our failures.

This is one of a series of books that we at Paraclete are publishing in our desire to inspire people to deepen their lives with Christ. In these books we will introduce you to the core life-principles of Benedictine spirituality, and demonstrate how our publishing mission is inspired by our life at The Community of Jesus on Cape Cod, Massachusetts.

Being genuinely interested in and concerned for others can be costly. It means putting the interests of others ahead of our own, even when we are tired, or we are just settling down to read a good book or to watch a favorite television program, or to take a nap, or any other anticipated pleasure. That's when hospitality begins to cost us our time and our comfort.

Hospitality is a kind of spiritual stretching; it sometimes forces us to become more limber. Like physical therapy: it doesn't always feel good. Getting involved with people can be a little frightening.

This book is all about looking to the interests of other people. And sometimes we do this at the expense of tending to our own interests. Hospitality is the crux of caring.

Still, it may come as a source of relief for you to know that others—certainly we—have to battle against undue self-concern every day. Each of us probably knows someone who seems to be so outgoing, so loving, so caring that it looks effortless. And for some, hospitality may actually come more easily. But "the good news of sin" (as someone once called it) is that we're all made out of the same human nature, and human nature is self-centered. So be assured that genuine caring, self-giving, and loving are the result of disciplined living, rather than some sort of innate craving to care for other people.

The Smallest Details of Hospitality—that become blessings when given to or for another person.

- Flowers
- Warm greetings
- Candles
- Words of encouragement
- Personal space
- An attentive ear and eye
- Beautiful (not just tasty) foods
- Personal notes
- A caring gesture
- Careful design
- Thoughtful music
- Time for silence

St. Paul wrote to one of the early churches:

■

If then there is any encouragement in Christ, any consolation from love, any sharing in the Spirit, any compassion and sympathy, make my joy complete: be of the same mind, having the same love, being in full accord and of one mind. Do nothing from selfish ambition or conceit, but in humility regard others as better than yourselves.

Let each of you look not to your own interests,
but to the interests of others.
—PHILIPPIANS 2:1–4

Hospitality is a powerful and wonderful way to live.
In these days, we need beauty more than ever before, and
hospitable actions are concrete ways of not only doing
what God asks us to do, but of spreading God's beauty.

Ours is a selfish age. We are accustomed to lighter
work loads than most previous generations dreamed
possible. We have more free time, and we want to be
entertained. Unless we do something active to break out
of this pattern, we will inevitably lead a basically selfish
life, even if we generate a veneer of pious feelings and
good behavior.

St. Paul, taking his inspiration from the life and
teachings of Christ, encourages us to have our faith
grounded in the One who did not hesitate to lay down
his life for us. He calls us to sacrifice our own interests to
his larger interests. This means putting others and their
needs ahead of our own.

For you were called to freedom, brothers
and sisters; only do not use your freedom as an
opportunity for self-indulgence, but through love
become slaves to one another.
—GALATIANS 5:13

Although to "become slaves to one another" sounds like drudgery—something we have to do—the openness and the love that accompanies a hospitable spirit is actually a path to a life of freedom. The more that we pursue God's desires, the more freedom and joy we will experience.

However, responding hospitably to others doesn't come naturally! But as we learn to prefer others to ourselves, we will discover that in giving, other things will be given to us. Jesus said in Matthew 6:33, "But strive first for the kingdom of God and his righteousness, and all these things will be given to you as well." When we willingly decide to practice loving our neighbors as ourselves, we find our own needs being met in new and unexpected ways. How do we love our neighbor as ourselves? The answer to that question is unique to each of us, but it is the crux of what it means to practice hospitality. Our answer to that question will come in how we respond to interruptions to our schedule today; in the way we respond to the needs of others as they are made known to us today; in the way we release or hold on to our own way—in any particular situation. These are some of the ways of showing hospitality. Loving self above all else, or loving our neighbor as we have loved ourselves—this is the choice that Jesus offers us.

❋

In *The Paraclete Book of Hospitality*, you will meet St. Benedict of Nursia, and be immersed in the spiritual environment that he formulated more than 1,500 years ago. Benedict wrote his now famous *Rule* for monastic life, drawing from previous monastic sources, to standardize spiritual wisdom for his community. To this day, this sixth-century document is the basic guide for hundreds of thousands of Christians, both laypeople and members of vowed monastic orders all over the world. *The Rule of St. Benedict* is the basic guide for monks of various orders (such as Benedictines and Cistercians), but is also the inspiration for today's neo-monastic movement. It establishes a way of life rooted in the gospel and grounded in the scriptural principles of charity, humility, and faithfulness. Benedict's rule sets forth an outline for Christian discipleship drawn from the heart of Jesus' ministry—the call to follow Christ, to be transformed by the work of the Holy Spirit, and to become living witnesses to the grace of God in the world. Every aspect of Benedictine spirituality is centered in this practical way of living for others—practicing hospitality.

As historian Carmen Acevedo Butcher, explains:

■

Benedict's careful attention in his Rule to explaining the monastic virtues of obedience, silence, hospitality, chastity, diligence, and non-violent behavior does suggest the man himself. Its simplicity is his own. The fingerprints of his humility are in every line of this spiritual guide designed—not for mystics or superhumans—but for the average person wanting to commune with God and enjoy a more meaningful life.

Its opening call to obedience (*Obsculta*) suggests that "holy listening" comes first but is indivisible from action. . . .

Listen, Child of God, to your teacher's wisdom. Pay attention to what your heart hears. Make sure you freely accept and live out the loving Father's directions. Working at obedience is the way to return to Christ when the carelessness of disobedience has taken you off-path. Follow Christ by wearing the strong, sacred shield of submission. Pray first before doing anything worthwhile. Then persist and never falter in prayer. God loves us as his own children, and forgives us, so we must not grieve him by rejecting that love and doing evil. We must always make the best use of the good things God gives us.

On every page we hear Benedict saying in this same caring, fatherly tone: "Pay attention. Surrender. Pray. Be kind. Stay humble."

❧

Well, the right thing to do is to keep the supreme Law of scripture: you will love your neighbor as yourself.

—JAMES 2.8 (NJB)

The call to love our neighbor as ourselves isn't limited to the words of Jesus. The first disciples and the early churches pick up the same theme and make love of neighbor the hallmark of Christian faith.

For the whole law is summed up in a single commandment, "You shall love your neighbor as yourself."

—GALATIANS 5:14

It was said of the early Christians: "Look, these people who call themselves 'Christians,' look at how they love each other!" When the early church fathers were preaching to the Greco-Roman world about Christian teachings, they often spoke of how Christians had come to love others as themselves. It was this quality that marked a person as someone who followed Jesus Christ. This new love carried them through the severest times of persecution, for they didn't "love their lives more than their faith." In other words, they did not love themselves and their own lives above others.

Every measure of sacrifice calls for loving others better than self, putting the interests of others ahead of our own.

The *Jerusalem Community Rule of Life* (a modern monastic rule) makes clear that hospitality has its roots ultimately in the incarnation of Christ, and that it is also a way to better understand the mystery of the Trinity:

God became man so that in man you might discover God. When you welcome men you meet God.

Whoever receives a man, in fact, receives Christ and whoever receives him in that very way receives the One who sent him.

By this very fact he actually meets the Father whom no man has ever seen. In a wonderful way hospitality and sharing lead you to contemplate God.

Since God is also himself hospitality and sharing, by following this rule you act like him and are led in a wonderful way to imitate him.

That is why hospitality has always been held to be a typical monastic virtue. Silence, fervor, penitence, and solitude are not enough. Only love is the supreme good.

Ask the Lord to make you grasp this mystery.

Often, feelings of guilt keep us from practicing hospitality. The following thoughts may freeze us into inactivity: *I haven't been hospitable in the past as I should have. I haven't responded to others in their time of need. Remember that occasion just recently when I saw a need and deliberately turned away? I was too busy.* The guilt builds up, one such occasion upon another, and before we know it, it's not so much that our hearts have hardened, but we don't know how to break out of our self-defense to change for the better.

Our hope is that this book will be an encouragement and guide for you to start anew.

And if you fail to respond to someone today, then tomorrow is the time! Forgive yourself, and accept God's forgiveness and move on. Otherwise, discipleship stalls, just waiting for the "right" time.

Throughout this book, all scripture quotations are taken from the New Revised Standard Version, used by permission, unless otherwise noted immediately after the Scripture quotation. Occasionally we have also retained the headings used by the NRSV when quoting longer passages. Excerpts from the *The Rule of St. Benedict* are taken from *The Rule of Saint Benedict*, translated by Abbot Parry OSB, introduction by Esther de Waal (Herefordshire, UK: Gracewing, 1990).

We would like to hear from you. Please send us your thoughts, responses, and insights about how we all can become people who practice a joyful hospitality to those around us. We may use your ideas in a future edition! Write to us at:

> Hospitality in Life
> Paraclete Press
> P.O. Box 1568
> Orleans, MA 02653

QUESTIONS FOR REFLECTION AND DISCUSSION

When he was asked to identify the most important question in life, Albert Einstein once answered, "Is the universe a friendly place or not?"

What do you think?

How might your answer influence your practice of hospitality?

ONE

Welcoming the Stranger

Sr. Bridget Haase is a storyteller, author of a warm and wonderful book, *Generous Faith*. She once lived in the remote Appalachian hills of West Virginia.

As a nun, Sr. Bridget seemed to give to others all the time with a fairly natural ease. She was good at it; as a nun, it was sort of her job. But Sr. Bridget gave to others from the heart, not out of obligation. She tells the story of a Thanksgiving when she became the stranger who was welcomed, rather than the one who was doing the welcoming. She reflects on how such an experience allows us to understand what it means to offer hospitality to others.

■

It was a Thanksgiving etched in memory.

For several months, I had been living in Sandy Lick Hollow in the hills of West Virginia, sharing life and lessons of the heart with my mountain-folk neighbors.

Delena and Elam lived two miles deep in a hollow. The dirt road, muddy, rugged, and often strewn with fallen branches, made my trip there both a challenge and a risk. I often wondered how they were ever able to get out, never mind how often.

"Home" was a ramshackle dwelling, hardly worthy to be called a "house." It was there that Delena and Elam raised their five children and a host of stray animals in need of shelter.

Their destitution was accentuated by cruel judgments and a mountain prejudice. They were shunned by neighbors who deemed them unfit and callously referred to them as "poor white trash."

Early one evening in late October, Delena and Elam came to visit for the first time. . . . "We'd be rightly honored if you would join us for Thanksgiving dinner. You're a long way from home, and it's a family day. We're asking early 'cuz we'd like to plan."

Filled with uncertainty, doubt, and longing, Delena's eyes caught mine.

"I am delighted with your gracious invitation," I replied. "I'll be there."

"Bring nothing. Nothing at all," called Elam as they got back into the truck.

Thanksgiving Day arrived. It was cold but snow-free as I began the trek to the hollow and to a holiday dinner with friends.

Pity for their situation overwhelmed me as I entered their home. There was no water, no electricity, no indoor plumbing. Flattened cardboard boxes taped together formed the walls that encircled the family and kept the winter cold at bay. The coal stove, intended to heat all the rooms, actually heated only one.

The children squealed with delight when I arrived. They ushered me in to "sit for a spell" to warm up and to catch up, so I took my place close to the coal stove. Delena said it was good to feel the warmth of life and blessings on such a day as this.

"Come to the table," Elam invited.

We all gathered around, held hands, and offered prayers of thanksgiving for all we had been given—our ongoing friendship, enough food, the children, the creek and abundant well water, summer pole beans and sun-ripened tomatoes, purple irises on the hills and blue chicory along the roadsides, the wood for the stove—and all that was yet to come. Then we took our places.

As I looked at my place, I could see that Delena had neatly arranged the best plate in the house, a Mason jar glass, a spoon, and a fork. She, Elam, and the children shared the remaining two plates, three forks, and two Mason jars.

My eye caught the decorations for such a festive occasion. Some sprigs from a pine tree spruced up an old jar. The cardboard walls facing me were decorated with pine cones and fir branches and held a boldly written message: "A big welcome to the church lady."

As soon as Elam offered me a plate with some sort of meat covered in oil, I sensed a challenge.

"Good, strong, wild meat," he said. "Been savin' it for just such a time."

I helped myself to the unidentified dish, knowing it couldn't stay on the plate and hoping it would stay down. I thought it best not to ask what made the meat strong and wild.

Then Delena offered me "the last greens picked before the frost got 'em all, and the mushrooms are from the summer. They been stored real good and should be fine."

I am sure she did not say "should be fine" in the emphatic way it sounded.

The meal went on. Eating, laughing, singing together a spirit-filled rendition of "The Old Rugged Cross" made thoughts of turkey, cranberry, and pumpkin pie oozing with whipped cream disappear into the cold air, and the reality of mystery meat and stale mushrooms find a resting place.

Before long, darkness began to set in and with it the time to take leave. It was the good-bye that I will never forget. Extending her hands, Delena took my hands in hers. Elam and the children surrounded me.

Delena began.

"We have somethin' to say before you leave. Hain't never, I mean never, has anyone done come to our home to eat with us. Not that we hain't invited them. But you came. And you came on Thanksgiving."

Then she paused, her eyes glistening with gratitude and penetrating mine.

"No," she continued, "it wasn't you. Today Jesus himself done come to our home, and we give thanks for the blessing of his presence. We don't have to go anywhere else to look for him 'cuz he is right here, before our eyes, inside our home. We look upon him."

I could say nothing. Delena and Elam, the poorest of the poor, the outcasts, had welcomed me as Jesus, had seen Jesus at their table and in their home. They knew that they were not born 2,000 years too late. They needed neither angel choirs nor a star in the East to proclaim his presence. Like an awkward drummer boy playing his instrument, they worshiped Jesus with the best they had, having found him in a church lady far from home on a holiday.

And then Sr. Bridget asks, "When have I humbly realized that someone saw Christ in me? How did this open my eyes to the beauty of sharing and to the witness of love?"

✻

Hospitality is spirituality moving outside of ourselves. So much of our spirituality is focused inward—on us, what we need, what we should do, what practices we're trying to learn or keep more faithfully, and so on. Hospitality means a lot of things, but all of them are chiefly about other people, not about us.

Christians didn't invent the notion of welcoming the stranger. Along with the Hebrew Scriptures (that we usually call the Old Testament), we inherited it from Judaism. In fact, we see many instances of the People of Israel practicing hospitality throughout the Old Testament. "In Hebrew, this is *hachnassat orchim*, literally 'the bringing in of guests,'" explains Lauren Winner, author of *Mudhouse Sabbath*. And, as was common, Jewish writings could be quite specific about what needed to be done:

■

Later rabbinic literature surrounds the biblical stories and models with codes and instructions. Rabbi Yochanan insisted that practicing hospitality was even more important than praying. Some rabbis turn hospitality into architecture, urging faithful Jews to build houses with doors on all four sides so that travelers and guests might find a welcome door from any direction. Many Jewish communities adopted the idea of serving all their dinner courses at once; this way finicky guests would not have to suffer through an appetizer or bowl of soup they did not like.

Early Christian communities continued these practices of hospitality, attempting to feed the poor, host travelers, visit the imprisoned, invite widows and orphans to join them at mealtime—all expressions of a capacious notion of hospitality. A second-century Christian text known as the *Didache* instructed Jesus' followers to help visiting travelers "all you can." In a sermon on Acts, renowned fourth-century preacher John Chrysostom told heads of houses not merely to delegate hospitality to their servants but to "personally welcome those [strangers and guests] who come" to your home. In the sixth century, Julianus Pomerius (sounding a little like Rabbi Yochanan) insisted that hospitality took precedence over other spiritual disciplines: he enjoined his readers to break a fast and "unbend one's self" in order to share a meal with others. The apostle Paul placed such a high value on hospitality that he listed it—along with temperance, sobriety, and gentleness—among the characteristics required of leaders of the church.

The Customary (or Rule) of the Order of Julian of Norwich includes these instructions: "the guest quarters in every House of the Order should in general be the nicest parts of the House. They should be immaculately clean, with everything in good functionary order, comfortable, and free of clutter."

We attempt to follow the same principles and guidelines in our lives at The Community of Jesus. This doesn't mean that we're interested only in showing our "best face" to those who visit us; it simply means that our orientation is toward others, toward any person who may come for a meal, for an overnight stay, someone with a special need or request.

We aren't all called to be monks or nuns, but hospitality is something that Jesus tells all of us to do. Our Community tries to do this within the tradition and context of Benedictine spirituality, inspired by Benedict's Rule.

The sixty-sixth chapter (the chapters are all very short) of *The Rule of St. Benedict* is an instruction to the porter, or doorkeeper, of a monastery:

■

At the gate of the monastery, a wise old man is to be posted, one capable of receiving a message and giving a reply, and whose maturity guarantees that he will not wander round. This doorkeeper should have a cell near the gate, so that persons who arrive may always find someone at hand to give them a reply. As soon as anyone knocks, or a poor man calls out, he should answer "Thanks be to God" or "God bless you." Then with all the gentleness that comes from the fear of God, he should speedily and with the warmth of charity attend to the inquirer.

Even something as specific as a medieval monk writing to other monks about how to answer the door has application for our homes today:

■

"All who present themselves are to be welcomed as Christ," writes Benedict.

"When did we see you?" asked the disciples.

Perhaps "every day" is the answer. At the door and in the neighborhood and at the corner. At the breakfast table and in the backseat and on the bus. In the break room and the grocery store. Naked and lonely and sick and imprisoned and thirsty and hungry covers a lot of ground, you know.

Benedict calls us to a constant awareness that those who enter our world are all to be treated as though they were the Christ. He calls us to a posture, a way of seeing and of welcoming and of serving, that is rooted in the sense of adoration of the Christ that is present in us all.

He calls for particular honor and care to be given to the poor, the sick, the needy, the guest, and the pilgrims. And who among us, who among those we know, who among those we shall meet tomorrow is not some or all or each at some time or all of the time?

The Rule calls us to order our lives and to maintain a sensibility for others that keeps us aware of and reflects the presence of the Christ among us always. Whether they live down the hall from us or are yet a stranger to us does not matter. The Christ among us is always to be honored, in things both great and small.

—ROBERT BENSON

Our Community guesthouse is called Bethany. One of our founders and her husband had owned Bethany and ran it as a bed-and-breakfast until the early 1970s. The first women she employed there to help serve her guests were to become the first vowed sisters of our monastic-style Community. It was in and through the ministry that took place in Bethany that our Community was founded.

In the gospels, Bethany was where Mary, Martha, and Lazarus lived. Jesus visited and ate meals there. According to tradition, he stayed there after his entry into Jerusalem on what we now celebrate as Palm Sunday. So Bethany is a place where we, too, try to practice some very special hospitality.

Meet Sister Sharon. She is one of our vowed sisters at The Community of Jesus. She has lived here most of her adult life, and her particular gift is hospitality.

Sr. Sharon embodies much of our own particular style of hospitality: how we respond to our guests and strangers. Hers—and ours—is certainly not the only way, but it is our way, given to us by God after many years of thoughtful reflection, listening, and prayer.

As Sr. Sharon is quick to explain, Bethany Retreat House is not only a place to escape from the pressures of the world, it is much more than that. If we are doing our hospitality well, guests will experience with us a wholly different positive atmosphere, not just be helped to escape from something. Our aim is to welcome guests by surrounding them with beauty and order.

Sr. Sharon says that every guest at Bethany comes with personal needs, but it is uncommon for them to articulate these things verbally. She tries to discern what would make each guest most comfortable by asking God to show her how to care for each person.

Some people need a beautiful floral tea cup, others a sturdy coffee mug that they can wrap their hands around. Not long ago, I served a guest whose father had recently passed away. I had a sense that I should set the breakfast table with china we seldom use. It was decorated in sprays of violets. At the end of the meal, this particular guest told me how much the china meant to her, as her father had given her violets each year on her birthday.

In the beginning God created. And he did it in an orderly manner. First came the heavens and the earth, next the light, dry land and the seas, and so forth. He didn't plunk down some vegetation, add an animal or two, toss in some fish, and say, "Oops, forgot the water!" He carried out a perfect plan that provided for and allowed each creation to flourish. His garden was beautiful. Each creature was known by name. When we create a home, and offer it to others, this is the sort of template we should follow.

Guests at Bethany are sometimes going through personal crises. The beauty and order that they find here is intended to enfold and surround them. We hope that they will feel loved and cared for without a word being spoken. My childhood was chaotic. I cling to order like a drowning man to a rope! It enables me to sort through myriad emotions and arrive at solutions.

Beauty and order is our philosophy of hospitality at Bethany Guest House. We try and create a place where the noise and clutter of the world are absent—an inward space where God's voice can be more easily recognized.

—SR. SHARON HUNTER

Hospitality Practices

- Offer a warm greeting to guests
- Be sensitive to people who feel awkward and shy
- Ask questions and listen
- Always try and have fresh flowers visible
- Keep everything clean
- Plan ahead
- Remember special needs and likes
- Invite people who will make each other feel comfortable
- Take people in as if they are already friends
- Recognize Christ in other people
- Give simple but meaningful gifts
- Add special touches—caring gestures
- Anticipate needs
- Practice simplicity and keep everything in its place.

When people come to Bethany, we thank God for bringing them, and we thank God for what he will do for them while they are with us. We anticipate that God is working in their lives, and we believe that since they have come to stay with us, we must be part of God's working in their lives.

While guests are with us, we go about our business while affirming God's love and care for them and God's activity in their lives. Sometimes we get to see or hear about the results, other times we don't. It doesn't really matter. It is a very satisfying experience to be able to pray for people in this way, but we are careful not to tell God what he should be doing for them. God knows, and that's enough. Our job is simply to open our doors and our life to guests.

On one occasion, a guest left a lovely box of chocolates for the Sisters who care for Bethany, and with it a card that read:

■

How can I tell you all that is in my heart as I leave this place? I came here empty and despairing. I was received and cared for in a way I had never before experienced. Leaving now, I'm still not without pain, but because of what I've received while here, my heart is full and I feel strengthened to go thru the healing process that lies ahead of me. I was hungry and you fed me, a stranger and you took me in, and somehow my life will never be quite the same.

There's a large picture on the wall in the stairway of Bethany Retreat House showing Jesus walking on the road to Emmaus.

According to the gospels, on the same day that Jesus rose from the grave, two of the disciples were walking toward a village that lay seven miles away from Jerusalem. These two already knew what had happened earlier that day—that Mary Magdalene had found the tomb of Jesus empty.

"While they were talking and discussing, Jesus himself came near and went with them, but their eyes were kept from recognizing him."

Jesus asks them, "What are you discussing. . .?" And they reply with just a bit of sarcasm to this "stranger":

"Are you the only stranger in Jerusalem who does not know the things that have taken place there in these days?"

And the two disciples told Jesus, thinking he was just an ordinary stranger, of all that had happened in the last three days.

Jesus then responded by explaining: "beginning with Moses and all the prophets, he interpreted to them the things about himself in all the scriptures." Since these two disciples were Jews, Jesus was teaching them from the Law and Prophets like a good rabbi would. But, in this case, he was teaching them about himself at the same time!

Finally, as the three of them approached the village of Emmaus, Jesus began to walk on as if he hadn't yet reached his destination—but the other two begged him to join them. They were practicing hospitality as good Jews would, saying to Jesus, "Stay with us, because it is almost evening and the day is now nearly over." They were inviting him to their table as well as into their home.

And then comes the climax of the story. . . .

"When he was at table with them, he took bread, blessed and broke it, and gave it to them. Then their eyes were opened, and they recognized him" (Luke 24:13–31).

This story—known as the "Walk to Emmaus"—gives us a great example of hospitality. Welcoming the stranger is the same as welcoming Christ himself. Here the stranger is Christ himself who awaits a hospitable invitation before he reveals himself in the breaking of the bread.

Look for the face of Christ in each person you meet. Then welcome him into your home, into your life.

QUESTIONS FOR REFLECTION AND DISCUSSION

Is it easier for you to show hospitality to strangers or mere acquaintances than to good friends?

Why?

TWO

Giving Yourself Away

*For, as I can testify, they voluntarily gave according to their means,
and even beyond their means, begging us earnestly for the privilege
of sharing in this ministry to the saints—and this, not merely as
we expected; they gave themselves first to the Lord and, by the will
of God, to us.*

—2 CORINTHIANS 8:3–5

The apostle Paul wrote these words to the church
in Corinth to describe the actions of the churches
of Macedonia: Philippi, Thessalonica, and Berea. If any
group of people could have pleaded that it was unable to
help others, it would have been one of these groups. The
fledgling churches in Macedonia were notoriously poor.
They had also undergone severe persecution at the hands
of the Romans. Paul seems to be genuinely surprised at
their generosity in giving toward the needs of their fellow
Christians in Jerusalem. Paul knew that there could only be
one explanation for this: they "gave themselves" away.

Consider what it means to give yourself away. Don't we
usually hold on to parts of ourselves, and only give when
its easy and comfortable? Sometimes we give to those to

whom we feel a duty or responsibility, often out of guilt. But giving ourselves away is more than giving money, or giving out of guilt. Money is often the easiest, least costly thing to give. Giving of our time, our interest, our concern, our energy, our personal space—these are usually far costlier ways because they involve giving ourselves away.

Jesus praised the poor widow who put everything she had in the treasury of the temple. He praised the woman who anointed his feet with precious ointment. We have honored brave pioneers, saints, teachers, soldiers, trailblazers—people who didn't hesitate to give themselves away.

Consider in your heart in what ways you might be called, with God's help, to give yourself away through hospitality. Once you've done that, the specifics will become clearer. Although you may be reluctant to take the first step; although the thought of giving yourself away in some new, untried, or unfamiliar way may seem threatening, in taking those steps you will find that Jesus becomes your companion. You will "see" him anew.

Lauren Winner explains: "Having guests and visitors, if we do it right, is not an imposition, because we are not meant to rearrange our lives for our guests—we are meant to invite our guests to enter into our lives as they are. It is this forging of relationships that transforms entertaining into hospitality."

At Home

Let's get specific. What are some simple ways that we can practice hospitality today, or this week, with friends, family, and maybe a few others, in our homes? *The Paraclete Book of Hospitality* is full of practical ideas. But like a good menu, here are a few starters:

- Show hospitality to the people who live in your home this week. Do something new and fresh to make them feel welcome, even in that familiar place. Fresh flowers in the bathroom. A small gift left on a pillow before bedtime. Come up with your own ideas, inspired by prayerfully considering the needs of those around you.

- "Break bread together" at dinner some night this week. Literally! This expression is a biblical one, and refers to sharing a meal together (see Mark 6:41, Acts 27:35), as well as to the way that Jesus shared a common loaf of bread with his disciples at the Last Supper (see Matthew 26:20–30). This latter way of understanding "breaking bread" shows how sharing a meal can also be a kind of worship. The sacrament of the Eucharist was begun at the Last Supper by our Lord; but there is also a sacramental aspect to sharing a loaf of bread with others. So instead of using presliced bread or rolls, try serving a loaf of whole grain, high fiber bread from which people

can tear off a piece. Then read together from one of
the Bible passages mentioned above.

- Another idea is to ask each person to share a prayer
  concern—or better yet, a reason for joyfulness—as
  he or she passes the loaf on to the next person.

- At a meal this week, try something different when
  you say grace: put a written prayer of thanksgiving
  at each person's place—something that you value
  in that person—and take turns reading each one
  out loud. You'll be amazed at how this can start a
  meaningful conversation.

- Return your attention to the works of mercy—first
  mentioned by Jesus himself in the parable of the
  Last Judgment. These seven things are concrete
  ways that the people of God should show hospitality by giving of themselves:

  Feeding the hungry
  Giving drink to the thirsty
  Sheltering the homeless
  Clothing the naked
  Visiting the sick
  Visiting the imprisoned
  And burying the dead.

Try to find a way to practice at least one of these seven
things in the next week.

At times, hospitality—just like following Jesus—can be costly. We are called to give ourselves away to others—to forsake (sounds like such a harsh word, doesn't it?) other very worthy and important things if they stand between us and serving God and others.

Many monastic rules, including our own and the *Rule of Taizé*, quote this important passage from the teachings of Jesus—Mark 10:29–30:

∎

Jesus said, "Truly I tell you, there is no one who has left house or brothers or sisters or mother or father or children or fields, for my sake and for the sake of the good news, who will not receive a hundredfold now in this age—houses, brothers and sisters, mothers and children, and fields, with persecutions—and in the age to come eternal life."

∎

Hospitality can be a kind of worship to God. True service to others seeks to bless and to extend God's shalom and goodness to the other person.

This kind of service is not servantile. It is not something that denigrates either the giver or the receiver. It is a service that makes the giver and receiver whole.

Service therefore is not us paying our dues. It is not a form of repayment. Service is not the tasks we are called to because God has blessed us and renewed us in Christ.

Seeking to serve and to be a blessing to others in whatever form that may take—witness, care, advocacy, prayer, giving, and the work of justice—comes from the love of God in us that recognizes the marks of God in the other person. This makes service worship. It makes it a sacrament.

—CHARLES RINGMA

Every day there are occasions, simple moments when we can show hospitality to another person by giving ourselves away. But like every valuable spiritual lesson, this one takes practice and focused attention on our part.

Robert Benson puts it well: "One does not have to go far to find Jesus. What one has to do is adopt a posture that allows one to see him." Still, there will be times when we are unable to see Jesus in the face of other people. At those times, we must work at changing how we see them.

Again, Robert Benson:

Christ is the old person next door, the one who fell on her steps in the dark and needs a meal every evening for the next month and has no family to prepare it for her. He can be found in the face of the sixteen-year-old who lives up the street, the one whose father is a crack dealer.

Christ is there in the tentative steps taken by that college student over there, the young girl who cannot find a friend.

He is there in the joy of the young couple down the street who are out every afternoon with their newborn in a stroller, just hoping that you will stop them and share in their joy.

My father used to say that when we get to heaven and see Jesus, our first thought is not going to be that we have never seen him before. Instead, we will grin and say, "It's you, it's you. I have seen you everywhere."

QUESTIONS FOR REFLECTION AND DISCUSSION

What are the toughest things—the toughest parts—of your life to give away?

Why do you think that you try to hold them back?

THREE

Caring for Others

L onni Collins Pratt and Father Dan Homan reflect in their book *Radical Hospitality* about the true meaning of hospitality:

■

Hospitality has two meanings for most people today. It either refers to hotels or cruise ships, or it is connected to entertaining friends and family in the warmth of candlelight with gleaming silver and ivory lace. . . . Benedictine hospitality does not allow us to turn people into a profit-making venture, nor are goodness and graciousness deemed suitable only for the cozy small world of our private homes and feminine natures. Benedict finds God in people. You can't ignore people when God is looking out their eyes at you. In the tiresome, the invalid, the rebellious, we are faced with God. It is our own failures to love that we have to deal with when we talk of hospitality.

Hospitality cuts through the sham of our excuses. Benedict is a realist about loving. He knows love comes only through effort and practice.

It is costly. It is fatiguing. It is not some warm, fuzzy feeling Benedict wants us to conjure up; he wants the strength of respect and reverence to beat in the hearts of his monks.

When we are filled with prejudice, suspicion, anxiety, or jealousy, we have no room for welcoming, for listening or receiving. The monastic life allows the monk to empty himself of the darker impulse, not that he is ever completely rid of it, but he actively resists in the sharing of the table and the embracing of strangers.

Hospitality did not begin with Howard Johnson's and *Good Housekeeping*. Hospitality, as it has been practiced from ancient days, protected people from the dangers of traveling alone. In Saint Benedict's day there were no safe and cheap shelters for travelers. Along the way people could be brutalized, robbed, wounded, lost.

Monasteries saved lives when they opened their doors to strangers. It was not about comfort and entertainment—it was about saving lives. A little dramatic? Well, it seems that way today when we have a Marriott on every corner, shelters for the homeless and the battered, and hostels around the world.

This spirit of saving lives is still at the root of monastic hospitality. To receive others is to expose myself to all sorts of frightful dangers of attachment and rejection. Hospitality acknowledges the vulnerability of being human, both my humanity and that of the stranger. Travelers, too (Benedict called them pilgrims), are prone to all sorts of dangers. On life's journey each of us is a pilgrim. We aren't sure where we came from and where we are going. We are vulnerable and we need each other.

※

Everyone knows what it's like to face the people who are difficult to love, or even like. Each of us is different, and my "impossible" person may be your most favorite one! But we all have trouble loving and caring for someone.

Facing impossible people is at the core of the Christian walk. As many a saint has said in the past: if we only did the most basic things we are asked to do by Christ, we would flourish as his followers. But it's so hard sometimes to do the most basic thing—what Christ called the second greatest commandment: love your neighbor as yourself.

A portion from the *Rule of Life* from the Society of St. John the Evangelist may be helpful at this point:

■

We are also called to accept with compassion and humility the particular fragility, complexity, and incompleteness of each brother. Our diversity and our brokenness mean that tensions and friction are inevitably woven into the fabric of everyday life. They are not to be regarded as signs of failure. Christ uses them for our conversion as we grow in forbearance and learn to let go of the pride that drives us to control and reform our brothers on our own terms

※

Don't be irritated by the brother who sings off-key.   —*Rule for a New Brother*

Pray constantly for those who annoy you.
        —*Rule of Colmcille (Columba)*

▪

LOVE FOR ENEMIES

But I say this to you, love your enemies and pray for those who persecute you; so that you may be children of your Father in heaven, for he causes his sun to rise on the bad as well as the good, and sends down rain to fall on the upright and the wicked alike. For if you love those who love you, what reward will you get? Do not even the tax collectors do as much? And if you save your greetings for your brothers, are you doing anything exceptional? Do not even the gentiles do as much? You must

therefore be perfect, just as your heavenly Father
is perfect.
—MATTHEW 5:44–48 (NJB)

The sayings of Jesus are so commonly heard, and so
rarely applied. Some people might say that it is in fact
impossible to follow these commandments, especially
when they have to do with facing impossible people.

❦

Impossible people are those we find it enormously
difficult to live with peacefully and productively. Such
people may bother us because they refuse to play "by the
rules," or maybe they bring out the worst in us. Sometimes
they are supersensitive to what we do, or do not, give them,
but then they are insensitive to hurts that they inflict on
us. At times, although we hate to admit it, we may find it
difficult to forgive some of the things they do to us. And
we may especially dislike the negative qualities they are,
for whatever reason, able to bring out of us.

But keep this in mind: we aren't doing ourselves, the
other people, or God any favors by being dishonest. Many
of us relate to impossible people on a false basis. We paper
over the differences, or explain away the things that we
don't want to face.

Our patterns of relating to others can become so dishonest, so detached from what is really in our hearts, that

our responses come only from our minds, and no longer from our hearts. We rationalize away our feelings, and as a result we stop listening to the Holy Spirit.

Consider this week how you might become more honest with yourself, your friends, a member of your family, and with God.

⋙

Sometimes, we become so dishonest with ourselves—so detached—that we wall ourselves off from real relationships to keep from being hurt or devastated by another person. We need to honestly face how impossible the person seems to be. Then pray for the person, and admit that we don't know how to handle the situation, and that we need help. Read and absorb the command of Jesus that we are to forgive—not just explain away, but forgive—the wrongs done to us. Recognize that honesty is the best way, even though it may be difficult to live out in real life. There are no genuine relationships without honesty.

There's one more thing: recognize that, in the minds or experiences of others, *you* may be the impossible person!

⋇

Let's get practical. Here are some concrete suggestions of what you can do, right where you are, to practice hospitality by opening your heart

- Follow the instructions of Christ and actually *pray* for your enemies—this includes everyone whom you avoid, dislike, disagree with. Hold them up to God without judgment—God loves them as much as he loves you—and thank God for them.

- If you find it particularly difficult to be charitable (let alone hospitable) to someone in your life, you might try posting a photograph of this person in your home or on your computer. Force yourself to include that person in your universe. Say hello whenever you see the photo. Welcome this person into your life.

- Look for Jesus in the face of each person. He is present in each of us, even the ones we may not easily like! If you are not someone who usually looks people in the eye, look them in the eye—particularly if you're having trouble seeing Christ in them.

- You've heard the saying, "If you want to be happy, then be a happy person." In other words, sometimes we have to will ourselves to become what we want to become. Find a way to open yourself or your home to the person you find most difficult to love. Don't worry that your motives are not entirely pure (because you still don't like the person), and trust God to change your heart.

Here's a new way to learn to become hospitable toward "impossible" people in your life: pray for them in color.

Sybil MacBeth has created an entirely new, left brain way to pray. She explains:

•

> In Matthew's Gospel Jesus tells us, "Love your enemies, bless them that curse you, do good to them that hate you, and pray for them which despitefully use you, and persecute you" (5:44, KJV). Now, that's radical hospitality! We usually want to avoid our enemies, to forget that they exist. Even saying their names gives them a prestige we do not want them to have. Respond to Jesus' instructions by praying in color for someone you do not like.
>
> [Praying in color for people you don't like] will probably not feel at all relaxing or playful. Writing the names of people you dislike or who dislike you can be a big step. When you are done, if you can stand it, hang the icon of your finished prayer in a prominent place. Whenever you see it, remember that person as a child of God.
>
> —SYBIL MACBETH

Learning to "pray in color" is simple. Rather than pray in your mind and with only words, you learn to pray with pens or markers or crayons—on paper. It's a way of expressing your desires to God in a different way. Praying in color is re-energizing the prayer lives of thousands of people as this new method becomes more known through Sybil's work.

❋

Opening our hearts to others requires honesty—with others, and with ourselves.

■

Self-knowledge is, as Bernard [of Clairvaux] often insisted, the basis of all compassion—which was the word that he used for what we would call empathy. If I accept myself then I am far less likely to be dismayed by the folly of others and far more likely to simply welcome them as they are.
—MICHAEL CASEY, OCSO

QUESTIONS FOR REFLECTION AND DISCUSSION

Think of one person whom you find it difficult to love. Now, think of one small way that you can show hospitality to that person sometime in the next week.

□ □ □ □ □ □ □

Food and Table

S r. Irene Psathas is also a sister at The Community of Jesus. She is a culinary expert, both for us, and for those who visit the Bethany Retreat Guest House. But her talent for preparing beautiful meals was not an inherent gift, nor was it something that she mastered in a culinary arts program—she's just a good listener.

■

I had chosen lemon meringue pie as a dinner dessert for a retreat meal. The closer the meal came, the less time I had to make the pies.

Unexpectedly, that afternoon some day-old berry pies were given to us by a local grocer. They could conceivably have passed as a mediocre dessert for the retreat. But try as I might, no matter how many times I felt inclined to settle on serving them, I couldn't bring myself to do so. I simply did not feel at peace until I decided that, regardless of the pressure involved, I would launch into preparing the homemade pies as originally planned.

Now, there was one man on this particular retreat who had been stony faced from the time of his arrival. From all outward appearances he was only enduring his time with us and benefiting very little, if at all, from anything that was taking place. Without dwelling on it, I prayed for him each time I noticed him.

I've always been persuaded that no one's coming to Bethany is coincidental—that there is a purpose behind every visit. God has something for every person, no matter how difficult or unhappy they seem to us. So I prayed that this man would receive whatever God intended for him.

Late one evening, he appeared at the kitchen threshold. I had to look twice to make sure it was indeed the same person! Obviously he had been crying—his eyes were red and swollen, but his face was soft with the faint hint of a smile at the corners of his mouth. With some effort to keep his voice from trembling, he had come to thank me for the fresh lemon meringue pie that was tart and runny, just the way his mother had always made it. He couldn't tell me all that it had meant to him, nor did he need to; some things are understood without ever having to be spelled out.

—Sr. Irene Psathas

There are very few people whose hearts are not warmed or touched through food. Perhaps that's the reason why Jesus so often used food as a way to express care and concern for others.

Jesus prepared a cookout on the shore for his friends who were tired and hungry from fishing all night. He saw to it that lunch was provided for the multitude that followed him. Jesus' first concern for the young girl he raised from the dead was that she be given something to eat. One of the last things he did with his disciples before the crucifixion was to call them all together for a supper, and he made himself known to them in the breaking of bread after his resurrection.

We're all being prepared for a heavenly banquet. Perhaps this is why Jesus and the Scriptures use food metaphors over and over again—to show the life-giving quality of food and table. So, when we come to the table, remembering stories such as those from the Bible makes it a little bit easier for us to see Christ in the person sitting across from us.

■

It is very compelling that before Jesus explained God's words, before he explained the beatitudes to the crowd, he fed them. Only after they were fed did he start to teach them.

—MOTHER TERESA

There are other reasons why the table is the first metaphor that people have to understand hospitality. It is at the table that we most commonly *share* with each other.

Isn't the table where our mothers or fathers first taught us to think of the person sitting next to us? We weren't supposed to lunge at the food in front of us, but rather to offer it to the person sitting beside or across from us. The table is still the easiest place to begin to open ourselves to others—both friends and strangers. In fact, as we see over and over again in the Bible, the table is the place where strangers become friends.

This well-known scene from the Old Testament is often captured in religious art such as icons, and is known as "The Hospitality of Abraham and Sarah":

■

The LORD appeared to Abraham by the oaks of Mamre, as he sat at the entrance of his tent in the heat of the day. He looked up and saw three men standing near him. When he saw them, he ran from the tent entrance to meet them, and bowed down to the ground. He said, "My lord, if I find favor with you, do not pass by your servant. Let a little water be brought, and wash your feet, and rest yourselves under the tree. Let me bring a little bread, that you may refresh yourselves, and after that you may pass on—since you have come to your servant." So they said, "Do as you have said."

—GENESIS 18:1–5

The story continues as we read to what lengths this couple went to entertain these strangers:

■

> And Abraham hastened into the tent to Sarah, and said, "Make ready quickly three measures of choice flour, knead it, and make cakes." Abraham ran to the herd, and took a calf, tender and good, and gave it to the servant, who hastened to prepare it. Then he took curds and milk and the calf that he had prepared, and set it before them; and he stood by them under the tree while they ate.
> —GENESIS 18:6–8

These three "men" were the Lord himself appearing as three persons, generally considered to represent the Holy Trinity. You've probably heard the expression, in one form or another: *Be kind to strangers, because they may, in fact, be angels!* This is an ancient Jewish tradition, and it's crystallized by the writer of the New Testament book of Hebrews: "Be not forgetful to entertain strangers: for thereby some have entertained angels unawares" (13:2, KJV). Invite strangers to your food and table.

Those three "men" who came to stay with Abraham seemed like angels. But in truth, they represented the Holy Trinity. Imagine turning them away from your door. It all began with Abraham's hospitality: when he met them on the road, bowed down to them, and asked if he could wash their feet—create a caring place for them to stop on their travels.

※

Sharing a meal doesn't have to be as significant as this. We may be attending to angels unawares, but not always! Sometimes we're just making soup and a sandwich.

> Lord of the pots and pipkins,
>   since I have no time to be
> A saint by doing lovely things
>   and vigiling with Thee,
> By watching in the twilight dawn
>   and storming Heaven's gates—
> Make me a saint by getting meals
>   and washing up the plates!
>
> Lord of the pots and pipkins,
>   please, I offer Thee my soul,
> The tiresomeness of tea leaves,
>   and the sticky porridge bowls!
> Remind me of the things I need,
>   not just to save the stairs,
> But so that I may perfectly lay tables
>   into prayers.
>   —CECILY HALLACK

One of Rachel Srubas's poems was inspired by the thirty-fifth chapter of *The Rule of St. Benedict*. This chapter urges the monastic community to share the responsibilities of the kitchen. Take turns serving, Benedict told his monks. No one is "too important" to take part. Srubas's poem shows how these rudimentary guidelines for a monastic community still make sense in how we might reimagine how and why we eat, and how our preparing food relates to God's gifts to us. What God has given us, we give to others: this is how hospitality makes practical sense in our lives.

KITCHEN EUCHARIST

A biscuit saved from breakfast
washed down by two gulps of juice
makes a quick, kitchen Eucharist.
Casserole for a choir bakes in the great glass pan,
noodles and gravy gently bubbling their prayers.
I peer into the oven's hot, orange mouth,
and my eyeglass lenses cloud over with steam.
Quilt-mittened, I remove the evening's
    hot concoction:
an offering to you of savory incense,
your gift to us of sustenance.

Here is another story from Sr. Irene:

■

We usually try to plan a meal of fresh cod for visitors coming to the Cape for the first time. Most everyone seems to enjoy it, simply broiled or baked with a lightly buttered, golden crumb topping. Unless we know that whoever is coming prefers a rich sauce or is partial to having it deep fried, we serve it one of the first two ways.

When Metropolitan Emilianos of Sylivria, a well-known bishop of the Greek Orthodox Church, first visited us, I knew he had been traveling and had not been in his native land for a good while before arriving on the Cape. I suspected that with his monastic background he would favor fish over meat and that he would be inclined toward simplicity in his eating. I also had the feeling that, being Greek, he might appreciate having cod prepared the way Papa always cooked it, the whole fish (head and all) slowly baked in a bed of onions, celery, green peppers, fresh tomatoes, and olive oil, and then allowed to sit in these juices, absorbing the flavors for some time before serving, so I opted for that way of preparing it. Since he is a genuinely humble man, I now know that I could have served him most anything and he would have been satisfied and grateful.

But I will never forget the light in his eye and the simple statement he made when he came to the table and sighted the Greek-baked cod.

"This," he said, shaking his head in amazement and holding out his hands as though he had been presented with the greatest of gifts, "makes me feel that I am now at home."

Sr. Irene concludes:

■

There are few things I find more rewarding than feeding people and giving them what I know they'll like, and it's impossible to determine who gets the most pleasure or blessing from it—the recipient or the giver.

This is true for all of us who give of ourselves to others in small ways: we receive gifts, as well. [For the complete recipe for Sr. Irene's Greek-baked fish, visit our website at www.paracletepress.com/hospitality.html.]

The table is a place where being hospitable is often easiest: we know how to prepare a meal and how to make it a generous expression of our faith and charity. We can also be creative, adding special touches that make gathering together more than simply sharing food. At the Community of Jesus, we love to try to do this as a regular part of our living together, and in our inviting others to join us.

QUESTIONS FOR REFLECTION AND DISCUSSION

Does your family have any cultural traditions centered around food and table?

Why is the sharing of food by friends and strangers together so important in history and today?

■ ■ ■ ■ ■ ■ ■

FIVE

The Seasons of the Year

M any Christian churches observe the seasons of the liturgical year: year after year the way in which they worship is structured around stages in the life of Christ. The seasons of the church year offer Christians an opportunity to experience the life and ministry of Christ in a very real way. Special feasts and celebrations are marked throughout the year. The original intention of such occasions was to share the good news of the day with the community at large. There are natural ways built into each liturgical season for practicing hospitality—both with the church and at home.

ADVENT AND CHRISTMAS

Each liturgical year begins in late November or early December with Advent, the preparation for the coming of Christ at Christmas. Christmas Day is actually the beginning of Christmastide, also known as the Twelve Days of Christmas. January 6 is then the fixed date for the celebration of Epiphany, or the visitation of the holy men from the East, and the marking of the beginning of Christ's sharing his message with all people, Jew and Gentile, shepherd and astronomer.

Sometimes the best Christmas gifts are the ones that we make ourselves. They can certainly be a thoughtful way of showing hospitality to others.

Consider this year how to come up with an appropriate Christmas gift for family, relatives, neighbors, and others— such as your mail carrier, the woman at the local gas station who sells you milk each week, the young couple on your block who have recently had a baby, or the teenager who shovels your walk or mows the grass. Give something of yourself. Sometimes food gifts work best of all.

A basketful of preserves, a basket of fresh eggs, apples from your own tree—all of these are ways of showing your care for others. If you don't have access to such things, you might try something like a spaghetti dinner basket containing sauce you made with last summer's tomatoes and seasonings, homemade bread sticks, and a bottle of herb vinegar. Coming during the busy holiday season when few people have extra time to prepare meals, such a basket will be warmly received.

In addition to the normal Christmas gift-giving, there are specials days in Advent that historically are marked by particular ways of hospitality.

For example, December 13 is St. Lucia day in some traditions—also known as the Feast of Lights. St. Lucia, or Lucy, lived from AD 283–304 and was an early martyr of the church. She was a joyful young girl and her feast day is a time for celebration. Surprise your family or office with a homemade loaf of St. Lucia bread. (Visit www. paracletepress.com/hospitality.html for a great recipe!)

There is another interesting custom that we still observe at The Community of Jesus during the week leading up to Christmas. It is based on a practice that originated in the parish and cathedral churches of Europe around the fourteenth century. In our evening service of Vespers, the *Magnificat* (also known as the "Song of Mary" and taken directly from Luke 1:46–55) is always chanted after the appointed psalms for the day. The antiphon, or introduction to the *Magnificat*, is intoned by the cantor, or song leader, and then chanted by all participating in the service. Each antiphon during the eight days leading up to Christmas refers to an Old Testament name given to Christ and is preceded by the interjection "O"—for example, "O Emmanuel," "O Adonai." Thus, these are referred to as the "O" Antiphons.

All seven "O" Antiphons—and their names for Christ
- December 17: O Sapientia (*O Wisdom*)
- December 18: O Adonai (*O Adonai*)
- December 19: O Radix Jesse (*O Root of Jesse*)

- December 20: O Clavis David (*O Key of David*)
- December 21: O Oriens (*O Morning Star*)
- December 22: O Rex Gentium (*O King of the Nations*)
- December 23: O Emmanuel (*O Emmanuel*)

It was customary in the fourteenth century to be invited to the home of the village canon, who had intoned the antiphon that evening, for a glass of sherry, in order to celebrate the coming of Christ. Over the years, this tradition has evolved into "O Antiphon" parties that amount to a little holiday refreshment—a kind of appetizer preceding dinner each day that week. You may want to try this yourself, and delve deeply into the rich meaning of each of these names for Jesus. In our Community, the cantor who intoned that evening's antiphon hosts the party and briefly shares some thoughts regarding that particular antiphon.

On January 6, the day of the Epiphany, try serving an Epiphany Cake—a cake into which are baked foil-wrapped slips of paper. Each one has one of the fruits of the Spirit from Galatians 5:22 written on it: love, joy, peace, patience, kindness, goodness, faithfulness. The finder will keep this slip into the new year. [For this recipe, and plenty of others, visit www.paracletepress.com/hospitality.html.]

⁂

Lent and Easter

As the church year progresses, we come to Lent, the weeks leading up to Easter. On Ash Wednesday, we remember the dust from which we come, and to which we shall one day return, and we prepare to participate in the forty days of testing that our Lord experienced in the desert.

On the Tuesday before Lent—Shrove Tuesday, or Mardi Gras, or Fat Tuesday—we eat and drink and laugh in ways that may seem inappropriate the following morning. It is common to eat pancakes for dinner on this "Fat Tuesday." The custom comes from the need to use up fat, eggs, and dairy products before the Lenten fasting begins the next day.

Lent has always been observed in The Community of Jesus as a time of preparation for Easter. One of the customs from our earliest days as a community was our weekly Lenten meals. As a help to understanding and appreciating the significance of these days preceding Christ's death and resurrection, we would share a simple meal of home-baked whole wheat bread, butter, honey, cheese, sardines, and boiled eggs. Sometimes we have used rough napkins, heavy pottery dishes and mugs, and no silverware. Or we have decorated the bare wooden tables with fresh fruit, figs, dates, grapes, and nuts that can be eaten as the dessert. Jugs of grape juice and wine were used for our beverages. People might receive a selected quotation or a word from Scripture at his place. Try this sort of Lenten meal together with friends or neighbors this year. These can be special times of sharing, particularly between generations.

Busy homes and busy families will find it a challenge to observe occasions such as Lenten meals in some of these ways. The best rule of thumb is this: simply do *something* special, something out of the ordinary, to mark the occasions that mean the most to you, and use them as opportunities to show hospitality to others. [Go to www.paracletepress.com/hospitality.html to see the complete recipe for Bethany Whole Wheat Bread.]

The week of Christ's passion provides us with another set of observances and ways of remembering. First we commemorate those unforgettable moments of Palm Sunday, when Jesus enters Jerusalem on an ass. Then the night of the Last Supper, also known also as Maundy Thursday, when Jesus offers to wash our feet, for he was the servant of all. Jeremy Langford offers this reflection on how a Maundy Thursday service gives us an opportunity to give to each other:

■

As the church transitions from Lent to Easter during Holy Week, it is common in liturgical traditions to reenact Jesus' washing of the disciples' feet on Holy Thursday. Each year it strikes me how reluctant people are at first to get their feet washed by the priest or others. Having your feet washed or washing someone else's feet is uncomfortable, humbling, intimate. Yet, it is also liberating. Inevitably, once enough brave souls line up to have their feet washed and to wash the feet of another, more and more people join in. Sometimes, the process can go on for what seems an eternity!

The washing of the feet provides a powerful metaphor for what community is all about: caring for others—even strangers—and allowing ourselves to be cared for by others at an intimate level.

Sometimes liturgical moments in church are designed to prepare us for creating sacramental moments in our lives for others later on.

Joining a tradition that many Christians have observed over the centuries, the Thursday evening of Holy Week has become a time for us at The Community of Jesus to have another commemorative meal together.

Like the Passover seder that is celebrated in Jewish homes, Christians can have a similar meal inspired by the tradition as it is currently practiced within Judaism. You can serve lamb roasted and sliced, unleavened bread (pita bread works nicely), bitter herbs (such as cooked and seasoned endive), and wine or grape juice. Eating some of the same foods Jesus and the disciples ate seems to draw us closer to him and to each other as we remember the events of Holy Week.

There are so many rich opportunities for symbolism in the foods you select—in the teaching opportunities for both children and adults, and in the way that you prepare and share such a meal. We often read the Scripture from Exodus 12 so the children, and all of us, can remember the Old Testament history of the Passover meal.

A PASSOVER SEDER MEAL

If you prefer, try inviting friends to your home for a more formal Passover seder meal. Jesus celebrated the Jewish Passover with his disciples. Many Christians remember this important event in the last week of the life of Jesus by hosting a Passover seder in their homes. You may even ask a local rabbi to come and help you and your guests understand the traditions. This is a great opportunity to share a meal that is so full of symbolism that it cannot all be included here.

But look to the slim book *Let Us Break Bread Together: A Passover Haggadah for Christians*, by Pastor Michael Smith and Rabbi Rami Shapiro. It will guide you step-by-step through the preparations and the rituals of a seder meal. You will discover there that the foods you prepare, discuss, and eat at your seder may well be ones that you've never heard about. Such as:

- Charoset: a mixture of apples, nuts, red wine, and spices. Pastor Smith and Rabbi Shapiro describe each of these foods and their meanings in the seder ritual. For example, charoset "symbolizes the mortar the Jewish slaves made in their building pyramids for Pharaoh."

- Zeroa: a roasted shank bone of lamb, or a neck of chicken. "Zeroa is symbolic of the Paschal lamb offered as the Passover sacrifice in Temple days."

- Baytza: an egg, hard-boiled and then roasted. "The hard-boiled egg was a reminder of the festival sacrifice held at the Temple in Jerusalem. With the destruction of the Temple (first by the Babylonians in 586 BC and later by the Romans in AD 70), the Jews began to associate the hard-boiled egg with mourning the loss of their Temple. Today the egg reminds all of us to mourn the suffering of all peoples trapped in the horrors of slavery."

- Karpas: a green vegetable, usually parsley, representing the return of life in springtime. "During the seder

the karpas is dipped in saltwater and eaten. . . .
The saltwater represents the tears of suffering that
become tears of joy when we move from slavery to
freedom."

EASTERTIDE

Easter Sunday is a wonderful time to have friends and
acquaintances over for brunch or dinner.

Your menu should include some eggs (they have long
been a symbol of resurrection and new life), and if you have
children in the house, painting eggs is a great (if messy!)
way to involve them in the meaning of the season—
painting and decorating them, and even giving them away.

Easter is also a perfect time for baking bread and for
sharing a gift of bread with someone who might appreciate
a touch of God's love. Jesus compared faith to the process
of making bread:

He told them another parable: "The kingdom of
heaven is like yeast that a woman took and mixed
in with three measures of flour until all of it was
leavened."

—MATTHEW 13:33

Foods such as eggs and bread provide opportunities for subtle and simple teaching about why faith is important in our lives. Visit www.paracletepress.com/hospitality.html for the complete recipes for a variety of creative bread options, such as:

 ■ Betsy C's Sticky Buns. Before Easter, you might even warm a friend's heart and stomach on St. Patrick's Day with a freshly baked loaf of Irish Soda Bread.

Other special touches that can make people feel welcome in your home on Easter:

■ Place lilies, daffodils, forsythia, and other spring flowers everywhere.
■ Create colorful place cards at each place around the table, adding to the festivity and showing how intentional you are about the presence of each guest.
■ Get creative with a dessert! For instance, try something like Daffodil Cake, a lemon, custard-filled angel food frosted with flavored whipped cream.

Sometimes these additional moments of thoughtfulness make strangers into friends.

ALL SAINTS' DAY

God walks among the pots and pipkins.
—ST. TERESA OF AVILA

All Saints' Day is an ideal time for soup, including all of those root vegetables that you've recently pulled from the summer garden, or that you suddenly find looking fresher than ever at your local grocery store. Fill your soup pot with a wide variety of good things, and invite others to join in sampling God's bounty.

This is also a great occasion for involving children in a memorable way of celebrating All Saints' Day: host a "Heroes of the Faith" party. Encourage your children to practice some hospitality of their own, and include at your party all of those elements that kids love—games, foods, and costumes.

Each child can pick a saint or hero or heroine, dress up like that person, and tell a little about that person's life. It's amazing what can be learned from just a little reading about the saints, and how real they soon become.

All of these occasions and others offer unique opportunities to share our home and table with others, using the hospitality of food in special ways. Each liturgical season offers a special opportunity to make hospitality unique. These are times when we can celebrate together with friends what is most important in our lives.

Questions for Reflection and Discussion

What were your favorite holiday traditions as a child?
What are your favorites as an adult?

To what new customs might you begin to welcome others on these special days?

■ ■ ■ ■ ■ ■ ■

Opening Your Heart

There is something even more basic to practicing hospitality than learning how to share our table. Being open about our personal lives is more difficult than sharing the mashed potatoes.

This is learning to open your heart.

My heart is open to others. This statement rolls off the tongue so easily, doesn't it? But then we realize how often in any given week we completely ignore other people. We're too busy to notice. Or perhaps, we become disdainful of inconsequential conversations and encounters with others when we become wrapped up in our own affairs.

With Christian hospitality there are no inconsequential meetings. Barbara Brown Taylor tells this brief anecdote in her new book, *An Altar in the World*:

■

"You saved eleven dollars and six cents by shopping at Winn Dixie today," [the clerk] says, looking right at you. All that is required of you is to look back. Just meet her eyes for a moment when you say, "Thanks." Sometimes that is all another person needs to know that she has been seen—not the cashier but the person—but even if she does not seem to notice, the encounter has occurred. You noticed, and because you did, neither of you will ever be quite the same again.

Every human encounter is holy.

❧

Listen to what the apostle Paul had to say:

∎

BEAR ONE ANOTHER'S BURDENS

Bear one another's burdens, and in this way you will fulfill the law of Christ. For if those who are nothing think they are something, they deceive themselves. All must test their own work; then that work, rather than their neighbor's work, will become a cause for pride. For all must carry their own loads. Those who are taught the word must share in all good things with their teacher. Do not be deceived; God is not mocked, for you reap whatever you sow. If you sow to your own flesh, you will reap corruption from the flesh; but if you sow to the Spirit, you will reap eternal life from the Spirit. So let us not grow weary in doing what is right, for we will reap at harvest time, if we do not give up. So

then, whenever we have an opportunity, let us work
for the good of all, and especially for those of the
family of faith.
—GALATIANS 6:2–10

Hospitality is the crux of being open with each other:
what greater joy is there than entering into another person's
life, sharing the pain and the joy, being accepted and
accepting the other as a brother or sister in the Lord. Surely
it is one of the great gifts God has given us. But many of us
don't do it easily. Paul elevates this part of our life in Christ
to the highest possible virtue. We hear more than an echo
of the words of Jesus, reminding us that we are to love God
with our whole heart, mind, soul, and strength, as the first
and greatest commandment. And then, love your neighbor
as yourself—the second greatest commandment.

In spite of improved means of communication, making
it easier than ever to be "in touch" with people, are we more
open with one another than ever before? Probably not. In
fact, the ease of getting in touch has probably made our
getting in touch more superficial than it ever was. The
human heart longs for friendship, companionship, love.
Being hospitable begins right here: with opening ourselves
to the other, and learning the joy that being open can
bring. Yes, we may get hurt from time to time. Being open
means that we are open both for the good and for the bad;
but there is a joy to being open that Christ understood
when he commanded us to do it. We become vehicles for

the Holy Spirit to bless everyone concerned, to begin to
know what needs are there, and to find comfort in the true
companionship of others.

Being open to each other makes sharing our table more
than simply sharing our dinner. To be open is to respond
to needs in ourselves and others. As Fr. Martin Shannon
explains:

The story of Adam and Eve reminds us that hiding
is "second nature" to us. But it also reminds us that
we were made for intimate fellowship with God and
one another, and that we will never be fully satisfied, we will never be whole, until we know once
again the bond of love that unites us. Can there be
any greater sense of fulfillment than what is found
in the deep and genuine sharing of pain and joy, the
mutual acceptance of one another with all our flaws
and failings, the confidence that we can know and
be known without any fear of judgment or rejection? Surely, this sense of communion is one of the
great gifts God has given the Christian family.[5]

Our generosity is a response to the needs of others. Both our giving and their receiving—or at other times and other circumstances it may become *our* receiving and *their* giving—are sacred.

The Revised English Bible got it right when they translated the first beatitude this way:

> Blessed are you who are poor,
> for yours is the kingdom of God.
> —LUKE 6:20

❋

Our faith is grounded in the One who didn't hesitate to lay down his life for us. Jesus gave himself in a way that we are—believe it or not—asked to give, too. We are supposed to give up our lives, and this means our self-interests, our wills, even our desires and dreams, to the single cause of following Christ. We are supposed to do first what he wants for us to do.

This is why St. Paul says that without the gift of love and charity in our hearts, we are worthless:

■

> If I speak in the tongues of mortals and of angels, but do not have love, I am a noisy gong or a clanging cymbal. And if I have prophetic powers, and

understand all mysteries and all knowledge, and if I have all faith, so as to remove mountains, but do not have love, I am nothing. If I give away all my possessions, and if I hand over my body so that I may boast, but do not have love, I gain nothing. Love is patient; love is kind; love is not envious or boastful or arrogant or rude. It does not insist on its own way; it is not irritable or resentful; it does not rejoice in wrongdoing, but rejoices in the truth. It bears all things, believes all things, hopes all things, endures all things. Love never ends. But as for prophecies, they will come to an end; as for tongues, they will cease; as for knowledge, it will come to an end. For we know only in part, and we prophesy only in part; but when the complete comes, the partial will come to an end. When I was a child, I spoke like a child, I thought like a child, I reasoned like a child; when I became an adult, I put an end to childish ways. For now we see in a mirror, dimly, but then we will see face to face. Now I know only in part; then I will know fully, even as I have been fully known. And now faith, hope, and love abide, these three; and the greatest of these is love.

—1 CORINTHIANS 13:1–13

Self-giving charity and real love don't come naturally.
They are gifts.

Jeremy Langford shares the following insight about
what true friendship demands of us:

■

I remember one of my seminary professors saying
people who were able to appreciate others—who
looked for what was good and healthy and kind—were
about as close as you could get to God—to the eternal
good. And those people who were always looking for
what was *bad* about themselves and others were really
on the side of evil. "That's what evil wants," he would
say. "Evil wants us to feel so terrible about who we are
and who we know, that we'll look with condemning
eyes on anybody who happens to be with us at the
moment." I encourage you to look for the good where
you are and embrace it.

Whereas traditional friendship (*philia*) is pref-
erential (to have a friend is to prefer one type of
person over another), Christian friendship (*agape*)
is universal, unconditional, and open to all. Likewise, while the golden rule—"Love your neighbor
as yourself"—is a good formula for living a moral
life, Christ goes further by challenging us to "love
one another *as I have loved you*."

Loving as Jesus loved is not an abstract concept;
it's an essential practice in the Christian life. Loving

as Jesus loved means loving others for who they are and helping them be their best selves. It means going out of our way to love those who are marginalized, rejected, discriminated against, teased, diminished. It means befriending God so that we can love the people God loves.

Baldwin of Exeter, a medieval monk and Archbishop of Canterbury, once wrote in a book called *On the Common Life:*

■

[Charity] loves to have things in common, not to possess them individually without sharing them. In fact, charity loves to share them so much that it is sometimes unwilling to reclaim good that rightfully belongs to it and that someone else has taken. Charity is generous and shuns disputes; it does not seek its own interests and has no wish to enter into legal controversy, when charity itself would be in danger. It prefers to be cheated than to perish; to suffer the damages rather than be awarded the costs. . . . Whoever has the utterance of wisdom or knowledge, whoever has the gift of work or service, whoever has any other gift, whether greater or lesser, should possess it as having been given by God for the sake of others.

QUESTIONS FOR REFLECTION AND DISCUSSION

Turn back to the brief anecdote from Barbara Brown Taylor (page 75). Reflect on how every human encounter is holy—and how you might do a better job of showing hospitality in Christian friendship in ways that you normally do not recognize.

SEVEN

More from the Bible and the Rule

Do not neglect to show hospitality to strangers,
for by doing that some have entertained angels
without knowing it.
—HEBREWS 13:2

■

The Rule of The Community of Jesus
encompasses all of the essential elements of how we try
to practice hospitality in our lives. We live a daily monastic
life, according to the rhythms of praying the Daily Office
and celebrating the Eucharist together. This is what binds
us together as a community. But it is the ways in which
we express ourselves to others outside of the Community,
through hospitality, that marks our homes and church as
places where Christ, and every person, are welcome.

The Rule of Life of The Community of Jesus reads:

■

Our work of ecumenism and our witness to the
love of God for the world are rooted in the idea that
all are welcome within God's house. The ministry of
hospitality compels us to make room in our hearts

as well as in our community for Christ's presence
in whatever form he comes, and especially in the
person of the guest or stranger. The welcoming of
visitors, therefore, is a service to be rendered by all
Community members.

We endeavor in various ways to receive and include
guests in the life of the Community without disrupting the
discipline and rhythm of daily monastic life that are part of
the Community's inherent identity. Guests are encouraged
to join with the Community in its public prayer.

❧ 𝒥 ☙

We are not hermits. In fact, we don't allow members to
become so focused on their own spirituality that the visitor
or stranger is neglected.

Many of the great religious leaders and saints over
the centuries have struggled with this as well. Early in his
ministry, St. Francis of Assisi asked two of his friends, St.
Clare and Fr. Sylvester, to help him discern: was he, Francis,
supposed to devote himself to a purely contemplative life,
like most of the monks of his day who had withdrawn from
the world, or did God want his life to be more actively
given to the service of others. Francis was drawn to the first
sort of life. Many of the great saints have been. But his two

friends confirmed God's will for his life: Francis was not to live as a hermit, but rather he was to devote himself actively to others.

Later in his life, we see St. Francis scolding some of his Franciscan brothers when they become too adept at practicing silence and contemplative prayer. We see him scold his closest friends at times, reminding them that their number one task is to serve others, and that by serving others, they serve Christ.

HOSPITALITY IN THE TEACHING OF JESUS

"When the Son of Man comes in his glory, and all the angels with him, then he will sit on the throne of his glory. All the nations will be gathered before him, and he will separate people one from another as a shepherd separates the sheep from the goats, and he will put the sheep at his right hand and the goats at the left. Then the king will say to those at his right hand, 'Come, you that are blessed by my Father, inherit the kingdom prepared for you from the foundation of the world; for I was hungry and you gave me food, I was thirsty and you gave me something to drink, I was a stranger and you welcomed me, I was naked and you gave me clothing, I was sick and you took care of me, I was in prison and you visited me.' Then the righteous will answer him, 'Lord, when was it that we saw you hungry and gave you food, or thirsty and gave you something to drink? And when was it that we saw you a stranger and welcomed you, or naked and gave you clothing? And when was it that we saw you sick or in prison and visited you?'

And the king will answer them, 'Truly I tell you, just as you did it to one of the least of these who are members of my family, you did it to me.'"

—MATTHEW 25:31–40

There are many very practical and "ordinary" things we can do in order to carry out the instructions of Jesus.

 ■ Take time in your day to comfort someone who is saddened. Better yet, take time to seek out someone who you think might be having a tough day or week.

■ Seek out a child, young person, or younger adult who may need your help and advice.

■ Go out of your way today to be open to interruptions. Go through your day as if you have permission to be late for everything.

- Treat a visitor to your place of work in a special way, as something more than an "appointment" or piece of work to get done. Try to treat such people today as if they are your honored guests.
- Listen to other people in ways that you do not normally do. When friends begin to speak, focus your attention on them.
- Be warm with strangers. Surprise them by your concern for what's happening right now. The cashiers and servers that come in and out of our lives everyday would love to see Christ in your face today.
- Ask a friend if you can help. Don't worry about embarrassing youself or your friend. You may be surprised how much your friend was wanting someone to reach out.

Who can forget the story of Jesus at Mary and Martha's house for dinner? Is Jesus' response to the two women—sisters who obviously were prone to disagree about what sort of hospitality should be shown to a respected guest—a statement *against* good hospitality?

■

Now as they went on their way, he entered a certain village, where a woman named Martha welcomed him into her home. She had a sister named Mary, who sat at the Lord's feet and listened to what he was saying. But Martha was distracted by her many tasks; so she came to him and asked, "Lord, do you not care that my sister has left me to do all the work by myself? Tell her then to help me." But the Lord answered her, "Martha, Martha, you are worried and distracted by many things; there is need of only one thing. Mary has chosen the better part, which will not be taken away from her."

—LUKE 10:38–42

Jesus gently admonishes Martha for worrying too much about the domestic details that seem to be taking her away from what is most important: the two commandments to love our God with all we have, and to love our neighbors as ourselves. This is a good corrective for all of us who practice hospitality: our motives should always be to serve Christ in the other, not to become the world's greatest chef, or to impress our guests with our attention to details.

❊

The story immediately preceding the story of Mary and Martha in Luke's gospel is that of the good Samaritan. Is there any better expression of what it means to care for a stranger than this?

■

Just then a lawyer stood up to test Jesus. "Teacher," he said, "what must I do to inherit eternal life?" He said to him, "What is written in the law? What do you read there?" He answered, "You shall love the Lord your God with all your heart, and with all your soul, and with all your strength, and with all your mind; and your neighbor as yourself." And he said to him, "You have given the right answer; do this, and you will live." But wanting to justify himself, he asked Jesus, "And who is my neighbor?" Jesus replied, "A man was going down from Jerusalem to Jericho, and fell into the hands of robbers, who stripped him, beat him, and went away, leaving him half dead. Now by chance a priest was going down that road; and when he saw him, he passed by on the other side. So likewise a Levite, when he came to the place and saw him, passed by on the other side. But a Samaritan while traveling came near him; and when he saw him, he was moved with pity. He went to him and bandaged his wounds, having poured oil and wine on them. Then he put him on his own animal, brought him to an inn, and took care of him. The next day he took out two denarii, gave them to the innkeeper, and said, 'Take care of him; and when I come back, I will repay you whatever more you spend.' Which of these three, do you think, was a neighbor to the man who fell into the hands of the robbers?" He said, "The one who showed him mercy." Jesus said to him, "Go and do likewise."

—LUKE 10:25–37

> Contribute to the needs of the saints;
> extend hospitality to strangers.
> —ROMANS 12:13

> [L]ove one another with mutual affection;
> outdo one another in showing honor.
> —ROMANS 12:10

This last exhortation can be difficult, and each Christian who tries to practice it struggles:

> Be hospitable to one another without complaining.
> —1 PETER 4:9

THE HOSPITALITY CHAPTER
FROM *THE RULE OF ST. BENEDICT*

Chapter 53 in St. Benedict's Rule is the inspiration for most of the Christian monastic tradition on the subject of hospitality.

All who arrive as guests are to be welcomed like Christ, for he is going to say, "I was a stranger and you welcomed me." (*The Rule of St. Benedict* 53:1)

As soon as a guest is announced he should be met by the superior or by brethren with every expression of charity. (*The Rule of St. Benedict* 53:3)

Special care is to be shown in the reception of the poor and of pilgrims, for in them especially is Christ received. (*The Rule of St. Benedict* 53:15)

QUESTIONS FOR REFLECTION AND DISCUSSION

Which of the phrases or portions of *The Rule of St Benedict*, chapter 53, seem most important to you?
Why?

EIGHT

Additional Passages from Monastic Rules of Life

A rule of life sets forth an intentional path consisting of specific steps that can be taken for the purpose of forming one's life around an ideal. The word *rule*, in this case, comes from the Latin word *regula*, which is also the root for words such as *ruler*, or *regular*—in other words, those things that are supposed to be models for behavior. A rule is not supposed to sound strict, but if it sounds disciplined, then you're hearing it correctly. Helpful rules of life are patterns that guide us to become people ready for heaven. Popular author Dallas Willard once compared a rule to a "Curriculum in Christlikeness"—and that's just about right. At the Taizé Community in eastern France, one of the common phrases used for hospitality is "A Face of God." Our actions of giving to strangers and guests literally show God's face in our world. This is so needed in our world.

The *Rule of Taizé* sums up our subject matter very well:

∎

It is Christ himself whom we receive in a guest. Let us learn to welcome; let us be willing to offer our leisure time; let hospitality be liberal and exercised with discernment.

The source of hospitality is the heart of God who yearns to unite every creature within one embrace.
—Rule of Life from the Society of
St. John the Evangelist

Be warm and merciful and let none go from you empty-handed. The least you can offer is your time and patience, your affection and your prayer.
—Rule for a New Brother

Our mission of loving service to our guests is . . . not found in developing chatty or entertaining relationships with them, or in showering them with constant attention, but . . . in disciplining ourselves and our needs in order to give them the gift of silence and solitude.
—The Customary of the Order of
Julian of Norwich

Be wide awake to the dangers of unlimited hospitality. . . . You might reach saturation point and end by becoming superficial, distracted, or monopolized. Do not be nowhere in your effort to be everywhere, or attentive to no one simply because you are running after everyone.
—Jerusalem Community Rule of Life

Be your genuine self. Then people will know you as you really are. . . . [L]et your life point the way to the source, and God himself will welcome.
—*Jerusalem Community Rule of Life*

Each one should confidently make known his need to the other, so that he might find what he needs and minister it to him.
—*First Rule of St. Francis of Assisi*

Welcome God. Unless you are God-filled there will be no sharing and giving; unless he lives in you, you will be unable to welcome people sincerely.
—*Jerusalem Community Rule of Life*

As the Father sees in every person the features of his Son, the firstborn of many brothers and sisters, so [we] with a gentle and courteous spirit accept all people as a gift of the Lord and an image of Christ. A sense of community will make [us] joyful and ready to place [our]selves on an equal basis with all people, especially with the lowly for whom [we] shall strive to create conditions of life worthy of people redeemed by Christ.
—*Rule of the Secular Franciscan Order*

QUESTIONS FOR REFLECTION AND DISCUSSION

Which of these quotations speak most closely to your heart, to the ways that you want to give to others?

Have you ever considered writing your own rule of life?

Creative Teachers and Teachings

The more that we help friends meet God, and the more we become comfortable offering this sort of support, the more we will be strengthened to welcome strangers with a similar purpose in mind.

CREATIVE RESPONSES—INNOVATIVE THINGS THAT PEOPLE AND COMMUNITIES ARE DOING TODAY

Lonni Collins Pratt, coauthor of, *Radical Hospitality*, tells the following story from her days of sitting in a hospital waiting room to illustrate what it means to hear another person's deepest needs.

■

When my infant daughter was being treated for cancer we spent a lot of time in a waiting room at Children's Hospital in Detroit. The babies and toddlers, the kids and the teens, all waited in that room for a turn at having chemicals put into a vein in the desperate hope of stopping cancer in its tracks. Parents, relatives, and friends waited with the children.

I was there with my little baby; often my father was with me. It's not spoken, but we have something like assigned seats in that place and somehow we all find out one another's story. I don't recall much talking about cancer, but we heard each other in other ways, ways I don't remember anymore.

On this particular day one of the chairs is empty and we all know what that means. It means one of us isn't coming back. One of us is gone. Another one has lost. That makes the waiting room quiet.

I'm not the only young mother in the room. There's one next to me with her son Matthew. Matthew is a year old. He's very thin with sticks for arms and legs. He has the largest eyes you will ever see on a child. He's bald. Most of the kids are bald. Chemo.

Across from Matthew is a teenaged girl, probably fourteen or fifteen. She, too, wears a stocking cap. Matthew's is red, hers is navy blue. The girl has been there since before Angie and I started in the waiting room. She's curled up in her chair in something like a fetal position. In any other place on the planet, people would be very concerned about what she is doing and how she looks. Here—well, here nothing is like anywhere else on the planet. She is with her aunt, because her single father won't go to the hospital with her. It is too hard for him to bear, he says.

Matthew's mother puts him on the floor. Show time. He pulls himself up to standing, using one of the orange plastic chairs to balance, and then he lets go and just stands there wobbling. He has our attention. When a child like Matthew does something as ordinary as take his first steps, it is good news in a place like this, a sign of hope. We cling to every crumb of hope.

The girl is watching. She doesn't want you to notice, but she's untangled those long, skinny arms and legs of hers and is slouched in the chair now, peering at wobbling Matthew from under her stocking cap. Matthew's sky-blue gaze fixes on the girl. He waves his arms and he's off—walking, really walking, while his mother beams at this never-before-seen event.

He takes seven steps to the girl. I count them. He bumps into her bony knees, slaps his hands down on her legs, and looks up at her with a great big grin and grunt of triumph. Magic. Her face is changing, transforming into a smile that reaches her young eyes and makes her pretty again. She speaks. Another first.

"Can I hold him?" she asks the mother.

"Sure."

She scoops up the baby into her arms, "Well, Mr. Matthew, aren't you something!" she says softly and snuggles him tight to her caved-in chest. He relaxes against her, tucks his head under her chin, and spreads his arms wide open around her shoulders. He takes a deep breath and exhales. He goes limp. They sit there like that, the two of them. It's hard to tell who is holding who.

Lonni reflects:

■

They have found their way home to each other. They have heard each other when no one said a word. Their connection is the same one we all share—our frail humanity. We do so need each other, and doesn't it terrify us?

With all its unforgettable beauty, this is still a sometimes dark and sometimes shuddering world we live in. We recognize this, no more profoundly than when we discuss such things as children living and dying with cancer, or the horrors of terrorism.

It is a courageous thing to keep getting up every day, and it is a much more courageous thing to rouse your heart and incline it to love. To care for each other, to open the door to the stranger, to open your heart to the stranger, lifts you up into the great dance of life.

There is a wider way, a higher way. To go this way we must keep our hearts open to the possibility of serendipity in the eyes of the stranger. God is among us. In a world where we see only in part and know even less, it is hard to spot God. Our eyes are not trained to see any better than our ears are trained to listen. It is not important that we recognize God in the stranger; God is there whether we notice or not. We can just assume that fact and do the next thing—accept the stranger. What matters is that we stretch our hearts open and draw near to each other. It is the way of hospitality, the way of life, and it is, in this remote place where we have awakened to find ourselves, the only way home.

Let us welcome whatever comes our way—a dying friend, a reclusive spider, a jewel-encrusted icon, the apothegms of Christ—and find in these gifts the beauty of all created things and of our God, who breathes them into being and upholds them through love.

—PHILIP ZALESKI

Hospitality is the virtue which allows us to break through the narrowness of our own fears and to open our houses to the stranger, with the intuition that salvation comes to us in the form of a tired traveler. Hospitality makes anxious disciples into powerful witnesses, makes suspicious owners into generous givers, and makes close minded sectarians into interested recipients of new ideas and insights.
—HENRI J.M. NOUWEN

Here are some ways in which ordinary people practice hospitality in ordinary ways.

Meet Karen Ward, Lutheran and Anglican pastor in Seattle and the founder of Anglicouch, a way for its members around the world to welcome near-strangers (you have to be a member of the online community of Anglimergent) into their homes. Anglicouch might just be a wave of the future, a way to link the interconnectivity of the Internet with real experience between people—in this case through offering simple expressions of hospitality to travelers. Anglicouch describes itself as "a way for Anglicans to get off the consumeristic grid by practicing and receiving the gift of no cost housing hospitality on the couches and in the guest rooms of Anglimergent members."

❈

Meet the Interfaith Hospitality Network of Athens, Georgia (www.ihnathens.org). This organization exists in order to help families in need throughout northeast Georgia. The Network is a coalition of fifteen area congregations that have partnered together. Similar organizations exist across the United States. For example, check out the IHN of Greater Cleveland (www.familypromisecle.org), or the IHN of Greater Cincinnati (www.ihncincinnati.org), or the IHN of Greater Denver (www.interfaithhospitality .org). The list goes on.

The IHN of Athens provides a community response to help homeless families in crisis situations achieve sustainable independence. The only requirement for admission into the Network is that the family is homeless and includes children. During the day, if the families are not working, at job interviews or at school, they reside at The Day Center, the main headquarters of IHN of Athens. This facility is a historic home owned by First Baptist Church of Athens, and can be used as a mailing address and phone number by these guests. The building also offers showers and laundry facilities.

At nights, the guests stay with one of the host congregations. Host congregations rotate as a place of shelter on a weekly basis, operating from Sunday to Sunday. At these congregations, volunteers provide meals, transportation, and lodging. These congregations include Methodists, Baptists, Lutherans, Episcopalians, and Unitarian Universalists. Hospitality brings these groups together in ways that are unusual otherwise.

Meet the folks at Holy Apostles Soup Kitchen, a symbol of hope and compassion in the Chelsea section of New York City since 1982. Housed in the Episcopal Church of the Holy Apostles, this soup kitchen serves about 1,200 hot meals every weekday, including holidays, welcoming anyone who comes in the door. Since the Soup Kitchen first began, it has served over six million meals! About fifty volunteers work in the Soup Kitchen program everyday. Their mission is to make sure that no one feels outcast or forgotten.

Experts tell us that the "St. Francis Prayer" that many of us learned even as children was not actually written by Francis of Assisi. In fact, it is anonymous and was written about a century ago. Still, the "St. Francis Prayer" captures the generous spirit of St. Francis in a beautiful way, and as we aim to become a joyful, welcoming people, it remains one of our favorites:

■

Lord, make me an instrument of Thy peace;
where there is hatred, let me sow love;
where there is injury, pardon;
where there is doubt, faith;
where there is despair, hope;
where there is darkness, light;
and where there is sadness, joy.
O Divine Master,
grant that I may not so much seek to be consoled
    as to console;
to be understood, as to understand;
to be loved, as to love;
for it is in giving that we receive,
it is in pardoning that we are pardoned,
and it is in dying that we are born to Eternal Life.
Amen.

QUESTIONS FOR REFLECTION AND DISCUSSION

Add your own story about creative ways to practice hospitality—and send them to us. We would like to hear from you at www.paracletepress.com/hospitality.html. Thanks!

Notes

7 *Benedict's careful attention in his Rule*   Carmen Acevedo Butcher, *Man of Blessing*, 87–88.

15 *It was a Thanksgiving etched in memory.*   Sr. Bridget Haase, *Generous Faith*, 119–123.

20 *Later rabbinic literature surrounds*   Lauren F. Winner, *Mudhouse Sabbath*, 45–46.

23 *"All who present themselves*   Robert Benson, *A Good Life*, 51–52.

34 *"Having guests and visitors,*   Lauren F. Winner, *Mudhouse Sabbath*, 50–51.

37 *Hospitality can be a kind of*   Charles R. Ringma, *The Seeking Heart: A Journey with Henri Nouwen*, 49.

38 *Christ is the old person next door,*   Robert Benson, *A Good Life*, 54.

41 *Hospitality has two meanings*   Lonni Collins Pratt and Father Daniel Homan, *Radical Hospitality*, 46–48.

48 *In Matthew's Gospel Jesus*   Sybil MacBeth, *Praying in Color: Drawing a New Path to God*, 90.

49 *Self-knowledge is, as Bernard*   Fr. Michael Casey, *Strangers to the City*, 119.

56 *Lord of the pots and pipkins,*   This is taken from the popular poem, "The Divine Office of the Kitchen" by the American poet Cecily R. Hallack, originally published in 1927. It has also sometimes appeared under the title "Prayer Hymn." Hallack died in 1938.

57 *Kitchen Eucharist*   Rachel M. Srubas, *Oblation*, 39.

67 *As the church transitions from Lent*   Jeremy Langford, *Seeds of Faith*, 130–31.

75 *"You saved eleven dollars*   Barbara Brown Taylor, *An Altar in the World: A Geography of Faith* (New York: HarperOne, 2009), 95.

78 *The story of Adam and Eve*   Fr. Martin Shannon with Carol Showalter, *Open Your Heart*, 15.

81 *I remember one of my seminary professors*   Jeremy Langford, *Seeds of Faith*, 48–49.

82 *[Charity] loves to have things*   Baldwin of Exeter, quoted (with slight edits) from *Spiritual Tractates 15*, by Baldwin of Forde, trans. David N. Bell (Kalamazoo: Cistercian Publications, 1986), 183–84.

99 *When my infant daughter*   Lonni Collins Pratt and Father Daniel Homan, *Radical Hospitality*, 279–82.

103 *Let us welcome whatever comes*   Philip Zaleski, *Recollected Heart*, 173.

104 *Hospitality is the virtue*   Henri J. M. Nouwen, *Wounded Healer*, 88.

Resources for Further Exploration

If a book is found in the following list, it is quoted in the text of *The Paraclete Book of Hospitality*. Specific page numbers may be found in the notes. A select few other books and resources are quoted, as well, and the full bibliographical information for each is found in the notes.

Benson, Robert. *A Good Life: Benedict's Guide to Everyday Joy*. Brewster, MA: Paraclete Press, 2004.

Bill, J. Brent. *Sacred Compass: The Way of Spiritual Discernment*. Foreword by Richard J. Foster. Brewster, MA: Paraclete Press, 2008.

Butcher, Carmen Acevedo. *Man of Blessing: A Life of St. Benedict*. Brewster, MA: Paraclete Press, 2006.

Casey, Michael, OCSO. *Strangers to the City: Reflections on the Beliefs and Values of the Rule of Saint Benedict*. Brewster, MA: Paraclete Press, 2005.

Haase, Sr. Bridget. *Generous Faith: Stories to Inspire Abundant Living*. Brewster, MA: Paraclete Press, 2009.

Langford, Jeremy. *Seeds of Faith: Practices to Grow a Healthy Spiritual Life*. Brewster, MA: Paraclete Press, 2008.

MacBeth, Sybil. *Praying in Color: Drawing a New Path to God*. Brewster, MA: Paraclete Press, 2007.

Nouwen, Henri J.M. *The Wounded Healer: Ministry in Contemporary Society*. New York: Image Books, 1979.

Pratt, Lonni Collins, and Father Daniel Homan. *Radical Hospitality*. Brewster, MA: Paraclete Press, 2004.

Ringma, Charles. *The Seeking Heart: A Journey with Henri Nouwen*. Brewster, MA: Paraclete Press, 2005.

Shannon, Martin, with Carol Showalter. *Open Your Heart: 12 Weeks of Daily Devotions*. Brewster, MA: Paraclete Press, 2008.

Smith, Pastor Michael, and Rabbi Rami Shapiro. *Let Us Break Bread Together: A Passover Haggadah for Christians*. Brewster, MA: Paraclete Press, 2005.

Srubas, Rachel M. *Oblation: Meditations on St. Benedict's Rule*. Brewster, MA: Paraclete Press, 2006.

Winner, Lauren F. *Mudhouse Sabbath: An Invitation to a Life of Spiritual Disciplines*. Brewster, MA: Paraclete Press, 2007.

Zaleski, Philip. *The Recollected Heart: A Guide to Making a Contemplative Weekend Retreat*. Notre Dame, IN: Ave Maria Press, 2009.

Rules of Life quoted in this book, in addition to *The Rule of St. Benedict:*

- *Jerusalem Community Rule of Life.* The Jerusalem Community is a relatively recent Roman Catholic order, founded in Paris in 1975 in order to bring the spirit of desert monastic spirituality to the great cities and urban places of the world. Quotations taken from *A City Not Forsaken: Jerusalem Community Rule of Life*, translated by Sr. Kathleen England. Foreword by Carlo Carretto. London: Darton, Longman and Todd Ltd., 1985. (Now out of print)

- *Rule of Taizé.* The Taizé Community was founded in the village of Taizé in Burgundy province of France in 1940 by Brother Roger Schutz. The life of the Taizé Community is aimed at demonstrating that it is possible for Christians of all denominational backgrounds to be united. Quotations taken from *The Rule of Taizé in French and in English.* New York: Seabury Press, n.d. 1968. (Now out of print)

- The *Rule of St. Colmcille* is an ancient Celtic rule of life. Quotations taken from *The Celtic Monk: Rules and Writings of Early Irish Monks* by Uniseann Maidin, OCR. Kalamazoo: Cistercian Publications, 1996.

- *Rule for a New Brother* was written for a religious community in the Netherlands by H. Van Der Looy. Quotations taken from *Rule for a New Brother* by H. van der Looy. Foreword by Henri J.M. Nouwen. Springfield, IL: Templegate, 1976.

- The *Rule of Life*. The Society of St. John the Evangelist, founded in 1866 in Cowley, Oxford, UK, is a monastic community of men serving the Anglican Church. They are sometimes called the Cowley Fathers, and have had houses in England, Scotland, India, South Africa, Japan, Canada, and in Cambridge, Massachusetts. The complete text of this rule is available online, at www. ssje.org.

- The *First Rule of St. Francis of Assisi* was written by St. Francis in 1209, the same year that he founded his new order and traveled with his first eleven companions to Rome to seek approval from the pope. Various editions.

- *The Customary of the Order of Julian of Norwich* is available online at www.orderofjulian.org. The Order of Julian of Norwich was founded in Connecticut in 1985, and its primary house is now in Wisconsin. It is a contemplative order within the Anglican Communion.

- *Rule of the Secular Franciscan Order.* Originally written by St. Francis of Assisi himself, this version can be found on the website of the National Fraternity of the Secular Franciscan Order—USA: http://www.nafra-sfo.org.

ABOUT PARACLETE PRESS

WHO WE ARE

Paraclete Press is a publisher of books, recordings, and DVDs on Christian spirituality. Our publishing represents a full expression of Christian belief and practice—from Catholic to Evangelical, from Protestant to Orthodox.

We are the publishing arm of the Community of Jesus, an ecumenical monastic community in the Benedictine tradition. As such, we are uniquely positioned in the marketplace without connection to a large corporation and with informal relationships to many branches and denominations of faith.

WHAT WE ARE DOING

BOOKS | Paraclete publishes books that show the richness and depth of what it means to be Christian. Although Benedictine spirituality is at the heart of all that we do, we publish books that reflect the Christian experience across many cultures, time periods, and houses of worship. We publish books that nourish the vibrant life of the church and its people—books about spiritual practice, formation, history, ideas, and customs.

We have several different series, including the best-selling Paraclete Essentials, and Paraclete Giants series of classic texts in contemporary English; A Voice from the Monastery—men and women monastics writing about living a spiritual life today; award-winning poetry; best-selling gift books for children on the occasions of baptism and first communion; and the Active Prayer Series that brings creativity and liveliness to any life of prayer.

RECORDINGS | From Gregorian chant to contemporary American choral works, our music recordings celebrate sacred choral music through the centuries. Paraclete distributes the recordings of the internationally acclaimed choir Gloriæ Dei Cantores, praised for their "rapt and fathomless spiritual intensity" by *American Record Guide*, and the Gloriæ Dei Cantores Schola, which specializes in the study and performance of Gregorian chant. Paraclete is also the exclusive North American distributor of the recordings of the Monastic Choir of St. Peter's Abbey in Solesmes, France, long considered to be a leading authority on Gregorian chant.

DVDS | Our DVDs offer spiritual help, healing, and biblical guidance for life issues: grief and loss, marriage, forgiveness, anger management, facing death, and spiritual formation.

Learn more about us at our Web site:
www.paracletepress.com, or call us toll-free at 1-800-451-5006.

Also in this series ...

The Paraclete Book of Balance

ISBN: 978-1-55725-667-6
$12.99, Trade Paper

Balance (noun): A PLEASING INTEGRATION OF
ELEMENTS; STEADINESS; EQUILIBRIUM.

This book of ancient and contemporary monastic
wisdom, practices, and reflection will inspire you to
integrate love for God, devotion to family and friends,
dedication to community, and desire for satisfying work—
in one, balanced, life. Chapters include:

- Is it *Really* Possible?
- How to Do It
- Finding Balance in the Seasons of the Year
- Balancing Prayer and Worship
- Balancing Work and the Rest of Life
- Reconciliation and Forgiveness

The result is an inspirational guide for practical living.

Available at bookstores everywhere
Paraclete Press 1-800-451-5006
www.paracletepress.com